MW01142006

THE THREE

LIFE

LEADERSHIP

LESSONS

THE THREE

LIFE
LEADERSHIP
LESSONS

Unfolding the Better You

LARRY MATEJKA

Pleasant W rd
A Division of WINEPRESS PUBLISHING

ISBN 1-4141-0831-1
Library of Congress Catalog Card Number: 2006907331

TABLE OF CONTENTS

Author's Foreword

I would like to first say that I am very thankful for the many leaders and leadership authors that have helped me grow to become a better leader. Fellow leader, I have no doubt that by this point in your life you have thumbed through and maybe even read hundreds of books on leadership principles. Awesome leadership books in which each author emphasizes a particular area depending on his or her personal experiences, gifts, and talents already fill our bookstores and libraries. Likewise, this book will also emphasize specific leadership areas. However, I believe it is meant to be that you are reading this specific book at precisely this time in your search for answers. I have confidence that if you act on just a few areas discussed in this book you will become a better leader.

There was never a particular moment in my life when I realized that I must pass on these lessons so others could learn from them. All my life I have been teaching lessons as fast as I could learn them. Everything contained in this book I have already taught hundreds of times.

Please do not be deceived by this, however. Just because I write about these leadership areas does not mean I am an expert at putting them into practice. To the contrary, it has been my tremendous struggle and failure in these specific areas that has given me a deeper understanding of these life leadership lessons. I have learned most of these lessons the hard way. I hope this book helps you avoid some of those same trials.

The three lessons in this book are presented in the order that I learned them. Each lesson will bring you to a new level of understanding and will probably leave you with some questions that the next lesson will answer. Upon completion of this book, I will send you out on a mission to improve your own life and the lives of others. I will send you out to lead in the gap, to make a difference, to be a world-changer within your own ten-foot circle.

Below are three separate models with each one representing one of the lessons (or chapters). Following, you will see the three assembled as one to make up the complete Life Leadership Lessons model.

Primarily, you need to remember the following: The arrow represents the plan used in the gap between your current situation and the better situation. You will see the arrow holds a place for three action plan items.

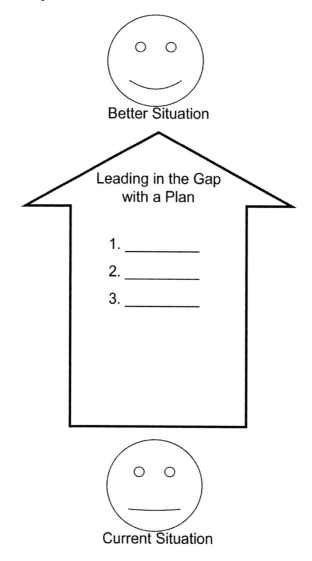

Better Situation

Leading in the Gap
with a Plan

1. _____
2. _____
3. _____

Current Situation

The star represents the light of truth that will ensure that you base your plan and make your decisions with good information (the truth).

The heart represents your motives of love that naturally create an environment of truth.

The complete Life Leadership Lessons model.

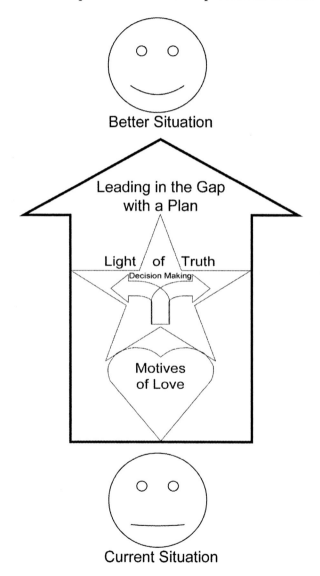

OVERVIEW

Lesson One: Leading in the Gap with a Plan

Better Situation

Leading in the Gap
with a Plan

1. _____
2. _____
3. _____

Current Situation

Highlights:

- We define the leadership role as any position that provides the opportunity to positively influence the lives of others in a lasting way.
- The people we need to lead are in our ten-foot circle.
- The three worlds in which we are meant to lead: self, family, others.
- Lead in the gap between the current situation and a better situation that you desire.
- Progress does not happen by accident. It must be purposeful. Develop an action plan, even if that plan consists of just three things written on a gum wrapper.
- Pain in the gap is good pain.

Lesson Two: Making Decisions in the Light of Truth

Highlights:

- The ability to make effective decisions is what closes the gap.
- A large portion of leadership is simply making decisions, but our decisions are only as good as the information upon which we base them. To base decisions on anything other than the truth will have dire consequences.
- Making decisions is like standing at a Y in the road and picking one branch to follow. Each branch of the road represents a choice in what lies at the end of that branch. Is it what I want? Am I basing my decisions on truth, feelings, traditions, or popularity?
- The truth tears down what is hindering progress and builds up what is helping progress.

Lesson Three: Motives of Love Create an Environment of Truth

Highlights:

- Why are you leading? What is your heart's desire? Whatever it is, the people whom you lead probably know your heart's desire better than you do. Motives project onto our faces like movies. Therefore, we cannot hide them.
- Whatever fills your heart will spill out of your mouth.
- Any motives other than love, caring, and the development of others will suppress truth or cause truth to hide from you. Truth is light. Without truth, you are bound to make decisions in the dark.
- Love opens ears, eyes, mouths, hearts, and minds. Fear shuts them.
- Love makes a way for truth to surface, to be audible, and to provide the basis for action.

INTRODUCTION

Over the years, I have been presented with many leadership challenges. These challenges ranged in size from a large retail company, to a single retail location, to a single department, to one-on-one coaching and counseling. These varied challenges are where I learned the three lessons of life leadership. Because I have no formal training from college or anywhere similar, life forced me to look at each of these situations in a very basic, simple way until I was really seeing them for what they were. I have always been focused—or maybe obsessed—on how to get people to maximize their potential. I have always concluded that people do not need to be *molded* as much as *unfolded*. It always turned out the potential was sitting there dormant and by repeating the same Three Life Leadership

Lessons, I could tap that potential:

Lesson One: Leading in the Gap with a Plan. If I could get a true picture of the current situation as well as the desired better situation or goal, then I could see the true gap (nature and size) that exists between the two and create a simple action plan with the steps necessary to close that gap.

Lesson Two: Making Decisions in the Light of Truth. But my decisions regarding what steps of action to take would only be as good as the information that I used to make those decisions. What makes the best information? The truth makes the best information. Therefore, I needed as much truth as I could get regarding the current situation—in terms of strengths and weaknesses—and as much truth as I could get regarding a clear vision of the desired goal or better situation. Truth is like light and once you get it and the lights come on, formulating the action plan is easy, almost a "duh" moment.

Lesson Three: Motives of Love Create an Environment of Truth. How would I be sure I could get truth from the people and be able to deliver truth and have the people accept it as well as not run when they heard it. It was all about my motives. Unless every person involved knew that my motives were to simply care for them, to help each person win, succeed, grow, and prosper, then I would never be able to get or deliver truth. I would always have to start by building relationships. I would always have to get to know the people and let them get to know me. I would have to talk out and walk out my motives of love.

Now, let us look at these lessons in reverse to see how they would work. As people would begin to believe my motives by what I said (the talking) and did (the walking), they would begin to share their truth with me and let me share my truth with them. As soon as we would start to make decisions on this truth, the gap would start closing as the current situation would start to move toward the better situation. Then, every time we witnessed forward movement or behavior–no matter how small–towards the better situation (the goal) we would *celebrate the victory*. We would praise/encourage one another, high five, pat each other on the back, or just let out a yell. Then, *momentum* would kick in and nothing could stop us. We would tap the potential–we would tap the *hidden 30 percent*.

A Testimony

Tapping the Hidden
30 Percent Potential

I believe we *all* have 30 percent potential hidden deep within ourselves and that potential gets tapped into when we love and are loved (lesson three), speak and hear truth (lesson two) and are in the truth about where we are and where we want/ must go (lesson one). People ask me, "If we have potential to be 30 percent better, better at what?" My response is "Everything or anything."

I work for a local sales/service company where sales are the ongoing focus. Our shared objective states, "To obtain our sales objectives through superior care of our employees and customers." In this ongoing focus on sales, our General Manager (my supervisor) does an outstanding job of driving marketing, products, operations, etc. For me, as the company's Organizational Development Director, my focus is primarily on the development of the people. I suggested to the General Manager that the company could get to the next level of sales performance if we tapped the full potential of the people. I was confident I could do this if I combined the Life Leadership Lessons material with the sales training. As it turned out, the class content was 80 percent on Life Leadership Lessons and 20 percent on sales techniques.

With the General Manager's permission, I pulled together the first group of eleven leaders—we have 80 total—and we discussed my approach for this two-day class. I explained that leadership is in essence the ability to influence others, and that the class members were going to learn how to better lead themselves and those reporting to them to attain significant performance improvements. In this particular group, each leader had from one to three managers reporting to him.

One of the first questions they posed was, "What specific area of sales are we going to choose to improve?"

"It doesn't matter," I told them. "Just pick something and we will improve it."

I then explained to them that the specific area of sales is not important; it is the leadership process that we will go through that is important. What process? The Life Leadership Lessons process. After selecting a sales area on which to focus, we worked through the Life Leadership Lessons process.

First, we all agreed that the objective of the class was to increase a specific sales area, but that the *number change* (improved sales number) would never happen without a *behavior change*. We all reviewed and agreed that the definition of insanity is, "To keep doing things the same way and expecting to get better results." The big question then became how to get the desired behavior change. We then proceeded to work through the Three Life Leadership Lessons:

Lesson One: Leading in the Gap with a Plan

1. We worked through the process of defining the *better situation* or the ideal future vision of the sales area. For this we chose to use best practices, which meant we used the sales number of the company's top performer in the particular area of sales as the goal or better situation.

2. We then worked through the process of defining the *current situation* to determine where each leader was performing currently in that same area.

3. We allowed the realization of the gap between item one and item two to really settle in for a few minutes. Then we did some exercises to look at what the impact would be on the company if 80 percent of our store sites were performing at the level of the best

practice site. The answer to that question meant that we would realize a huge profit increase. Once again, we allowed the gap between each manager's current situation numbers and the better situation numbers to really settle in. Now we needed to come up with a three-point action plan to close the gap. We started by analyzing what the best practice site was already doing.

Lesson Two: Making Decisions in the Light of Truth

4. We discussed packing the gap with truth. Truth about what? Truth about everything on this topic, starting with the truths that surfaced in each manager's own mind while doing Lesson One (this is what we call the two-foot circle which we will discuss later).

   Then, I told each participant, "If you just came to an understanding of the truth that you are not performing as well as you thought you were in this area and why, then enlighten those people within your ten-foot circle by saying that out loud right now in front of the class, and then go back to your store site and tell your entire team." We continued to search out every truth on the subject and the behaviors surrounding the subject. For example, how many performance behaviors were really driven out of fear and not truth. We discussed that fear-driven behaviors are seldom effective and if at all only short-term. These kinds of behaviors will never tap the hidden 30 percent.

Lesson Three: Motives of Love Create an Environment of Truth

5. I asked each participant, "What is your motive?" If it is only to improve sales as a way to improve a bonus check, I warned each of them that they would only go so far toward the desired improvement in sales. However, I added, "If your deeper motive is to truly help yourself and the others around you to win, to experience victories, to grow professionally and personally, and to improve their lives, then you will tap the hidden 30 percent." Love is the opposite of fear. I then told them to go back to their store site, invite a subordinate to breakfast, and then tell that person how excited you are about the class and then share these lessons with that person. "When you sit down, start by letting them know, first and foremost, that you care about them and want to help them grow and win." Let them know that you came to realize certain truths about yourself during the class, and that there are many improvements that you must make. Then share with them the vision of the better situation; let them feel

what it would be like if your store location were performing at the level of best practices. Then take them through a description of the current situation or current performance level and let them come to an awareness of the gap. Let them feel the "ugh" moment.

Finally, ask your subordinate what action steps they believe should be taken to close the gap. Then, describe what the best practice site has been doing to become the best practice site. Tell any truth you may have not shared in this area, including your frustrations, confusions, and lack of awareness. Be sure to share the good, the bad, and the ugly. Share all of it. Ask the person to do the same. Again, reassure them that your goal is to win, and to win together. Agree that you will both go out of your way to look for behavior changes in each other, no matter how small, and you will celebrate those victories daily. Do this knowing that you must both stay in the truth and watch the numbers because only the right behavior changes will change the numbers.

THE LIFE LEADERSHIP LESSONS RESULTS

Among the three geographic groups represented in the class, we realized an improvement in the selected area of sales of 31 percent, 32 percent and 35 percent. Below is the email that the General Manager sent out to each of our managers regarding the sales improvements:

Original Message

At 10:05 A.M. Sat, June 10, 2006, General Manager wrote:

Good Morning,

Congratulations to all on some awesome leadership victories regarding significantly improved sales performance following the recent sales training!!!!

Based upon the numbers, you absolutely accomplished the objective of seeing how much of an increase leadership alone could gain us in the chosen focus areas.

Without any additional advertising or even any internal manager special sales promotions, you achieved some unbelievable increases.

Bottom line is that you are projecting nearly $51,000 more in gross profits this June when compared to last June. If you can continue to execute on this level for the entire year, this means $600,000 more in annual gross profit!!!

Guys, I just want to share how proud I am of all of you for taking the leadership challenge and demonstrating the abilities to accomplish behavior change that results in significant sales performance improvements!!!

Thank you for all of your hard work. Let's keep the leadership moving forward. We will continue to track the numbers, and give you a weekly update.

As you can see, truth and love moves people. Now, let's move into our first lesson.

Lesson 1

LEADING IN THE

GAP WITH A PLAN

One can easily imagine the average person, as a driver, screaming down the road of life at eighty miles per hour. An observer flags the person down and the vehicle screeches to a standstill. Once the motor stops, the observer simply asks the person, "Where are you going?"

Evidently startled by the question, the person responds, "I don't know."

The observer then asks, "Where are you coming from?"

Again, startled by this second question, the person responds, "I don't know."

The observer then asks, "What is it that you do know?"

To this question, the person quickly responds, "Well, I'm making good time."

Do you sometimes feel like this person? Are you so busy getting yourself and others from one place to another place that were a casual observer to ask you where you are heading, would you be unable to describe it in two minutes or less?

First, let me say that you are not here to be molded. However, you are here to be unfolded. Most everything that you require in order to be an outstanding leader, you already possess. It is my belief that society has overcomplicated leadership. We must get back to the basics. My hope is that this book will act as a bulldozer that pushes back ineffective thinking and gets you down to the golden bricks of truth that will naturally come forth as you become more honest with yourself. I am confident our journey together through this book will be worthwhile and that you will come away from the reading experience a better leader than you are today.

Whatever your leadership responsibility—whether you are the chief executive officer of a multi-million dollar company, a Boy Scout troop leader, a classroom teacher, or the parent of three children—the leadership responsibility is the same. You must be responsible for the growth and well-being of others. Leadership is a massive responsibility that one cannot take lightly.

A New Definition of Leadership

The term leadership usually relates to the higher-level roles within companies and other large organizations. You may have never considered yourself in a leadership role if you are simply acting as a parent or if you have a small role in a local business with just one or two people reporting to you. I am going to suggest to you, however, that these are also leadership roles based on the following definition:

The leadership role is any position that provides the opportunity to positively influence the lives of others in a lasting way.

Leading is building up the lives of others. It is influencing people for their own well-being. If you have influenced people, then you are leading. If you live in such a manner that others around you are honestly able to say, "I'm better because of you," then you are leading.

We lead by stretching people to levels of behavior and performance that they never thought they could attain. When we do so, we are making long-term differences in those people's lives. The sad truth is, some people will never grow beyond the place that their leader believes they can go.

Yes, as leaders we have that much impact on people. Do not underestimate the impact you have on others.

If the leadership role is about helping others, then what about helping ourselves? Do we actually lead ourselves? Sure we do. We lead ourselves when we decide—consciously or unconsciously—what or whom we will follow. By our nature, we are followers. The people, experiences, and environment around us shape us. We make the choices about what we will follow and what we allow to influence us.

If, at this moment, you are not sure of what you are following, this book may help. Whatever you think about during the majority of each day, that is your leader. For example, I find that many people follow feelings instead of facts as they go about their day-to-day activities. If reading this book so far has not made you feel good, you may be thinking about putting it down. Please do not do so.

Followership comes before leadership. What or whom you follow has everything to do with the manner and the effectiveness by which you lead others. You cannot give away what you do not possess.

LEADING PEOPLE WITHIN YOUR TEN-FOOT CIRCLE

Who are we responsible to lead? Imagine that we have a ten-foot circle of impact around us in much the same way that an imaginary hula hoop encircles us and anyone else who happens to be within ten feet. What if some day we are accountable for the impact we make on all of the people who enter our ten-foot circle of impact?

Make a list of those people and prioritize your list starting with those who are most often in your circle to those least often. What do you see? Maybe your spouse was first and your barber, whom you have known for fifteen years, was last. I would imagine that you probably have no fewer than forty people on that list as you include family, friends, and neighbors. If each one of us were to take care of all of the people in our own ten-foot circle, and your circle overlaps with the ten-foot circles of everyone with whom you come into contact, it is conceivable that we could have an impact on every person on earth. Wouldn't it be nice if we could do just that?

Below you will see nine leadership roles that most of us typically try to fill all at once.

THREE WORLDS TO CHANGE

First—Leading self

1. Spiritual
2. Mental
3. Physical

Second—Leading family

4. Spouse
5. Children
6. Finances

Third—Leading others

7. Extended family
8. Friends, neighbors, acquaintances
9. Co-workers

Notice that they are categorized into three worlds or three areas with a very specific order of priority. In most cases, you will agree that it is very difficult to experience victories in one area of leadership if you have not done the proper amount of work in the areas that preceded it. As an example, the degree with which we succeed with our children (number five on the list) depends a great deal upon the success we are experiencing in our marriage (number four on the list). As you can see, there are certain principles of priority at work here. Principles such as, *You cannot give away what you do not possess.*

I find that many leaders do not lead themselves adequately. They lack self-discipline. They have unclear goals for themselves. They lack focus in their thinking and purpose in their actions.

If you want to bring about positive changes for others within your ten-foot circle, then you must first start by creating positive change within the two-foot circle that includes only *you*. This principle, of course, shows us that *it will be difficult to lead others if we cannot lead ourselves.* Because we are dealing with principles here, which we will talk more about in the next lesson, we find these principles defend themselves. If any of these principles are out of order, they will find a way to put themselves back into order.

For example, a man puts his job—the leading of others—first above all else. Very soon, however, he finds out that his wife is threatening to divorce him and then this causes his health to suffer so that eventually he ends up in a hospital with chest pains. As the man lies in his hospital bed, he begins to wonder how he became so confused as to risk losing his family because of a job. He also realizes that unless he takes care of his own health he will be no good at all to his family. He concludes, finally, that he must discipline himself to keep his job in third place, behind his own health, and the well being of his family. Thus, the principles rearranged themselves to their proper order all on their own.

The difference often is: Will your priorities rearrange themselves the hard way (like the above story) or the easy way because you took action on them? The hard way is the more common story.

My own experience, at one time, was exercising my best leadership skills at work (number nine on the list) while I ignored my friends and family (numbers four, five seven, and eight on the list). Finally, my health and inner peace (numbers one, two, and three) suffered. Eventually, everything came crashing down at the same time. I often counsel others by telling them, "If you put your career first, you are guaranteed to eventually lose it." Even though there are certain principles driving a priority here, a person cannot realistically expect to completely fix things at one level before he or she goes on to the next level. That is not how life works. Instead of nine different levels, I would prefer that you view these areas of influence and priority as nine boxes sitting next to each other. We work in all nine boxes at the same time, but we work at varying depths in each box depending on the season. We run into problems when we altogether ignore a box or two, as indicated in my previous examples.

We defined the leadership role as *any position that provides the opportunity to positively influence the lives of others in a lasting way.* We then reviewed our ten-foot circle of impact and all of our leadership roles to determine those whom it is our responsibility to lead. Now let us discuss where it is we are to lead them.

The Better Situation

Leadership is nothing more than influencing something or someone to a better situation. At this very moment you are *leading,* if you are working to help your child become better, your business to become better, your marriage to become better, or your church to become better. Whether you are trying to lead a large company with many employees or just one teenager, the process, by principle, is the same. You are essentially dealing with three elements:

1. The current situation that you want to make better (the sad face)
2. The better situation that is your standard or your vision of better (the happy face)
3. The gap between number one and number two (where we put the arrow/action plan)

Pain in the Gap

The gap is the place between where you are now (the current situation) and where you desire to go (the better situation). You do want to go somewhere, don't you? Do you want your business to go somewhere? Or your marriage? Finances? Health? And where is the place that you want all of these areas of your life to go? To the place of *better*! You want your business or your job to get *better*, your marriage to get *better*, your kids to behave *better*, your health to get *better*.

We all want to be moving closer to *better*. It is in our nature to progress, to move forward, and to grow. Maybe you call *better* your goal, your dream, your vision, or your purpose. Regardless of which word you use to describe *better*, it is *better*. Stop, close your eyes, and envision the ideal better situation that you desire and put together a movie in your mind. Process the movie frame by frame.

It is natural for us to want a better life. I believe God made us this way. Getting better is what challenges us to get out of bed each morning.

When you gripe about your marriage not being where you want it to be, or complaining about your business or your children, you are actually griping about gap pain. Gap pain is the pain that comes from awareness that the current situation is different from your vision of a better situation. From this we can conclude that not all pain is bad. There is good pain and there is bad pain. Knowing the difference between the two is critical to going forward. Gap pain is good pain and it can be used to do great things to help others.

Keep in mind that often we move our current situation closer to *better* in such a way that we close the gap until we raise the bar of our expectations and move our vision of *better* out even farther. By doing so, we again open the gap and this, in turn, brings back the pain. The gap will never go away as long as we keep pushing our dreams of *better* forward. However, if we understand the leadership process, then it becomes easier to turn that pain into something productive. We could define the word *gap* as an acronym for *griping about pain*. However, I truly believe that *gap* should more properly be an acronym for *God's Appointed Purpose*.

If you find yourself in one or more areas of your life standing in the gap between the current situation and a desired *better* situation, then I can guarantee you that you are being called to *lead in the gap*. There is no one else who can do that as well as someone who is aware of the gap. If you can *see* the gap or even *feel the pain* of the gap, then you can be sure you own all or a part of the responsibility for closing that gap. If you look at the people around you and you cannot understand why they are not as upset or as passionate as you are about the gap, it is probably because they do not see the gap. They may be called to close some other gap.

What about when we know something in our life is getting better. Awareness of a movement towards better tells us that we are on the right path, that we are OK and that our situation is going to be OK. Our hope returns. When something is getting better, it is a powerful fuel that we should then use to take us to the next level of *better*. When used properly, the hope that comes from moving towards *better* becomes an upwardly reinforcing spiral going from one level of our life to the next one, and then on to the next one, and so on.

What about when something seems stuck still and will not get better? It hurts even to think about such a thing. The situation seems to have a power over a person that he or she cannot overcome. At times, it may even seem as though that person is destined to failure. Such a situation can suck the life, the hope, the joy, and the energy right out of you. If such a thing is happening to you, you may simply decide that this is as good as the situation is going to get. You may find that the best way to relieve any pain of standing in that particular gap is to stop thinking that it can get better. When you do this, you are simply accepting the current situation for what it is in an attempt to relieve some of the pain. In such an instance, you have closed the gap not by moving your current situation closer to your vision of *better*, but by moving your vision of *better* closer to the current situation with a decision that the current situation and the better situation are the same. Do not be deceived by this, however.

Consider a particular area in your life and the gap between what it truly is now and what your picture of *better* is for that particular area. The gap looks large, doesn't it? The gap can close, however, and you are the only one who can do that task!

If just now in your own mind you heard, *Who am I to lead this situation or person to a place that is better?* then you need to ignore that thought and recognize it as a lie. Once we start believing that we cannot help others until we pull ourselves all together, we will never again help anyone. At this very moment, you already have an experience, wisdom, knowledge, or a resource that someone else desperately needs. Take note that the lie says you cannot help others until you pull yourself all together. The truth of the matter actually is you cannot pull yourself all together until you help others.

Maybe you heard an inner voice say, *I don't know how to lead.* That is another lie. You are already leading something. First, you are leading yourself. Second, you are leading anyone who is looking to you for guidance, comfort, encouragement, training, safety, stability, hope, food, clothing, shelter, etc. If you are not actively leading the people whom you are responsible to lead, then you are not releasing yourself from the responsibility of leadership, you are just not doing it well.

The entire world consists of pyramids of hierarchy: Family units, business units, government, churches, and associations. All of us are leading someone even as we simultaneously follow someone or something.

The act of leading others is not a choice. It is an assignment. However, *how* we lead others is a choice. Good leadership does not happen by accident. It is strategic. We do it on purpose. Good leadership requires thought and action. Lessons two and three in this book will show you what must be done to close a gap and move yourself and those you are leading to the place of *better*.

You must have an action plan! Even if this means that you simply write three things down on a gum wrapper because progress will not happen by accident!

As an example, I was once called to assist a district manager to bring about a change of attitude and performance at a specific office that our company had recently acquired. Several previous attempts during the past months had failed to bring about the desired change. During that period, the company's new employees became very disgruntled and the mood of the whole office was in a negative spiral downward. Negative creates negative and positive creates positive. This negative situation had really created an entire culture of negativity.

Once again, I simply followed my Life Leadership Lessons plan. Since most of the negativity was directed toward the acquiring company and not at any one person in particular, I decided to gather everyone into the same room and start a process of gathering truth. I brought my big easel, which always seems to frustrate everyone. However, I bring it because I believe it is important for everyone to see and work from the same piece of paper. This method is key to creating a pattern of unified thinking right away. If I were to go into a meeting with the idea of creating unity, the last thing that I would want to do would be to place the back end of a writing pad towards the other person with whom I am trying to work. This would only prevent that person from seeing what I was writing and surely not create any common ground from which to work.

I took my marker, I drew the Leading in the Gap with a Plan model I showed you earlier and I began to seek the truth by asking the group, "How would you describe the better situation or the ideal future vision of your present work location?" At first, this question frustrated them because all they could think about was their own specific problem and getting it solved. However, as they all verbalized the future in a way that was positive, hopeful, and better than where they were, it changed the whole atmosphere of the room. I wrote it down by the better situation. They heard each other and realized that they all wanted the same thing. They all wanted something better. Then I asked my second question. "How would you describe the current situation by giving examples of both its strengths and its weaknesses?" This is when they were able to "vent" all the problems. I wrote all that down by the current situation. After those two steps, the *gap* between the current situation and the better one became obvious. I then asked the group for the three things that in their minds would provide the strongest leverage to close the gap between the current situation and the better situation as they described. They immediately agreed on three items: (1) to fix a compensation problem that was an error at the time of the acquisition, (2) a work-flow problem that would require some behavior changes with several employees who agreed to these changes, and (3) a distribution problem that we could not fix short-term but came up with a strategy to overcome the obstacle in the meanwhile. I wrote that in the arrow. The whole process took about forty-five minutes. Within two days the performance from the location had increased.

ACTIVITY PAGE FOR LESSON ONE

Consider one particular area that you are trying to make better and write down three things that best describe the current situation, three things that best describe the better situation, and the three action steps that you have been considering to close the gap.

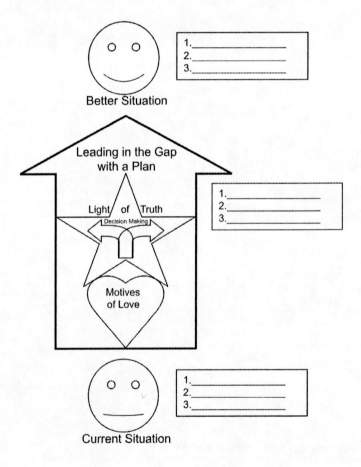

Better Situation

Leading in the Gap
with a Plan

Light of Truth

Decision Making

Motives
of Love

Current Situation

Lesson 2

. . . .

MAKING DECISIONS

IN THE LIGHT

OF TRUTH

I magine that someone presents you with the following challenge: A prize of $100,000 is waiting for you in an unknown place. A map that will guide you to the money will only be visible once you have assembled a 1,000-piece jigsaw puzzle. You have eight hours in which to assemble the puzzle and use the map to find the money. If you do not succeed, you must pay $10,000.

It so happens that you enjoy working jigsaw puzzles and often assemble them. You even consider yourself an expert. With confidence, you accept the challenge. After all, $100,000 is not bad pay for a single day's effort. Once the challenge begins, however, you are surprised to discover that each one of the 1,000 puzzle pieces is randomly buried throughout the yard. In order for you to assemble the puzzle, you must first search for each piece of the puzzle. You stand frozen in the yard not knowing where to start. You ask for release from the challenge, but the contest judges deny your request, but to ease the pain raise the cash prize to $200,000.

This makes you even more frustrated. Increasing the reward is not helping you see the puzzle pieces any better. After all, you still do not know where the money is until you have assembled the entire puzzle. You feel as if you are being stretched in two. Your desire to win the challenge is pulling you forward while the inability to see the assembled puzzle (the truth) is holding you back like an anchor.

Considering this analogy, now picture yourself standing in the gap between your current situation and a better situation. The map is actually your plan that holds the truth about those key decisions or actions necessary to close the gap. The pieces of the puzzle are pieces of truth buried in yourself as well as in the very people you are attempting to lead. You now must dig and get to your own truths as well as the truths found in those people surrounding you. If you can surface all of those truths, then assemble those pieces of truth into one overall truth, it is only then that the lights will come on and you will be able to clearly see the key decisions that you must make.

Does any of this sound familiar? You may have just signed on to a new job and you are feeling like it is presenting you with this very challenge. You desperately want to win, but you are lacking the treasure map. Maybe you are in a leadership challenge at home or at work and you feel as though you are operating in the dark. Your situation appears frozen and unable to move.

What makes the difference in how effectively we close the gap and move ourselves and those around us to the place of *better*?

MAKING EFFECTIVE DECISIONS

A good portion of leadership is nothing more than making decisions. We make hundreds, maybe even thousands, of decisions in a single day. Choosing the methods and selecting which decisions to make has everything to do with closing the gap between the current situation and the better situation. The decisions you make also will have an impact on the people we are leading, and any actions you take or fail to take might even affect their future.

Now we know at times that we must make big decisions in our business or home life. These decisions are big, obvious, and visible. They are not usually the decisions that cause us trouble because we tend to weigh these decisions very carefully. We create a process of gathering our information, weighing the options, and reviewing the pros and cons. However, it is the smaller, subconscious, and often unspoken decisions that usually land us in trouble. These less visible, split-second decisions are like many one-degree adjustments that, when all added together, make up a large change in direction that we do not begin to notice until it is too late.

When we make a decision, it is like being at a Y in the road and deciding whether to go to the right or to the left. We select a road and soon we find ourselves at another Y, and then another. We make one choice after another, road after road, with each road heading us in a particular direction.

If making decisions is like choosing roads, what makes us choose one road over another? What causes us to select one option rather than the other when making any decision? The answer is the source of the information that we are using to make our decision. Now this is very important because the information we gather and use determines our final destination.

Making decisions involves two basic steps:

1. Gathering information
2. Making a decision based on that information

In addition, the quality of the information gathered in step one determines the quality of the decision made in step two.

Therefore, your decisions are only as good as the information on which you base your decisions. Gathering good information—or better said, *truth*—is the only foundation to making good decisions.

Truth is like light. Light illuminates everything in the gap and lets us see things for what they really are.

Truth will expose false information and eliminate it from the decision-making process. Information that is true will stand firm and become the foundation for making the necessary decisions. Once we bring truth into the open, it is as if someone turns on the lights and we are able to stand back and say, "Duh, now it is clear what will be the best decision!"

As we continue in the gap with this process of getting to the truth and making decisions on this truth, we find that our current situation quickly starts to move toward the better situation. Wherever there is confusion, there is usually a lack of truth.

The best leaders believe with great confidence that there is such a thing as *truth* and that they will never have *all* of it. They know that the truth that comes their way, no matter how good or bad that truth may be, is revealed for a reason. The revealing of truth is a lesson, and each truth revealed is a lesson that we must learn. *We must catch the lesson!* The best leaders know that only powers beyond them hold *all* the truth. On the other hand, they also believe that there are ways to discover much *more* truth than they currently hold.

They are or they become truth-seekers. They will do whatever it takes to get to the truth. They know that the leader who gathers the most truth is the leader who usually wins. They know that to the degree they are in the truth, they will succeed in moving the current situation to a better one. They know that their *most* effective decisions are based on the *most* truth because their decisions are only as good as the information that they use to make those decisions. They are decisive. They do not suffer from paralysis of the analysis. They create an environment that will promote truth (we will discuss this in the next lesson), to get as much truth as they can, and then make a decision. The decision may not be perfect, but they are aware that by making a decision they will create more truth.

How is that? How do they create more truth? They seek truthful feedback on what worked and did not work in regard to their original decision, and then they use that additional truth to help them make the next decision. *Sometimes one must use a flashlight to find the light switch.*

MAKING DECISIONS IN THE DARK

Sometimes we make decisions in the dark. We choose a road and never consider where the road leads. We choose a road and do not realize we also choose what is at the end of that road. We make decisions in an almost unconscious state and then, usually after a significant event, we sort of wake up one day and say, "How did I get here to this point in my life?"

It is as if every time we choose a road, we choose the road leading south. Then, one day we start complaining because we do not like hot weather. We cannot figure out how we ended up in a place that is so hot. It could be as small a thing as deciding as you lie comfortably in your bed late at night that you are just too tired to get up and give your teenager the consequences because he just arrived home many hours after his designated curfew. When you choose that road, you choose what lies at the end of that road.

At other times, we do slow down and consciously gather information before we choose to make a decision based on that information. However, the information we gather is not the truth because it comes from bad information sources. Bad information sources do not give us truth. The opposite of truth is a falsehood or a lie. Lies are not real. However, lies can cause us to take action in much the same way as truths, especially if we believe that these lies are actually truths. We respond to what we believe is real much as a dog will bark at its own image in a mirror or a bird will fly into a large picture window because the bird only sees a reflection of the sky. Even if the lie tells us *not* to act, any decision *not* to take action is, in fact, an action. As truth creates light, so do lies create darkness.

Three common sources usually give us information that is *false*, even though we might think of it as the truth. I am not saying that these three sources cannot provide good information at times. However, I find that they most often give us bad information and we often overuse these unreliable sources. Imagine making important decisions regarding our families, our businesses, and our futures and basing those decisions on bad information.

Most people make the same decisions if using the same information. Most people do not use good information.

THREE BAD INFORMATION SOURCES

The three sources that often give us bad information:

1. The *majority* when used as an information source.
2. The *past* when used as an information source.
3. Our *feelings* when used as an information source.

Let us look at each one of these information sources more closely.

The *majority* as an information source: We assume that there is some validity or weight if the majority says something is true or right. It is a form of peer pressure on a grand scale. It is as if a mistake is not a mistake when enough people make the same mistake. It may be what is most popular at this moment. It may be whatever the media is screaming about the loudest. It is trends, fads, and advertising. Very often, it is our own cultural environment.

The *past* as an information source: We assume it is true or right because, "That is the way we have always done it." Instead of the word *we*, try substituting any of the following: the family, the company, and the church. Just because your parents did it, it must be right? Wrong! Traditions have the weight of many years driving them, but that does not mean that they are right. Habits formed over the course of many years often give us information that we subconsciously use for making decisions. We also use poor role models just because they were in our close vicinity during those most impressionable years.

Our *feelings* as an information source: Feelings are probably the most commonly used source of bad information. Why? You do not have to go far to get that information. It is the quick and easy way. In a time-impoverished society, feelings may appear on the surface to be the best way to proceed. You do not need to set a meeting, confront a family member, try to translate the meaning of someone's words, seek through a series of questions, do research, go to the library, do a survey, humble yourself by asking those wiser than yourself, or even make a phone call. You just reach in, grab your feelings on the matter, and run with them to make a decision. The problem is our feelings toward a certain matter may not have a darned thing to do with the truth. If we are using feelings when picking a road, we will pick the *path of least resistance* almost every time—the path that will inflict the least pain because we usually believe the lie that *pain is bad*. Yet, if you really think about it, our most significant growth and maturity usually comes from pain. Can you imagine a body builder using the *path of least resistance* method to enlarge his or her muscles?

As destructive as is the belief that all *pain is bad,* so is the corollary belief that all *pleasure is good.*

Emotions Affect Decisions

Look through this list of feelings and consider how these feelings can influence how you make decisions. These same feelings or emotions can also create walls of division that we will discuss later. Circle the words you can immediately identify with, so that you can refer to them when doing another exercise at the end of this chapter.

Anxious	Excited	Enthusiastic	Proud
Ashamed	Concerned	Disappointed	Discouraged
Dull	Embarrassed	Gloomy	Low
Moody	Quiet	Sympathetic	Useless
Worthless	Cold	Crushed	Isolated
Lonely	Offended	Pathetic	Suffering
Peaceful	Obedient	Comfortable	Annoyed
Awkward	Bitter	Confused	Angry
Enraged	Frustrated	Furious	Irate
Provoked	Resentful	Stubborn	Bold
Brave	Confident	Courageous	Daring
Determined	Encouraged	Heroic	Impulsive
Humiliated	Regretful	Guilty	Convicted
Independent	Loyal	Reassured	Secure
Absorbed	Curious	Fascinated	Defeated
Evasive	Distrustful	Helpless	Hesitant
Disobedient	Happy	Spirited	Timid
Hopeless	Indecisive	Perplexed	Pessimistic

Powerless	Skeptical	Unbelieving	Wavering
Alive	Empty	Hollow	Paralyzed
Sluggish	Stretched	Strong	Tense
Tired	Uptight	Weak	Weary
Aggressive	Close	Loving	Passionate
Warm	Bored	Cruel	Distant
Envious	Humble	Jealous	Preoccupied
Torn	Awed	Cautious	Cowardly
Dependent	Doubtful	Fearful	Scared
Hesitant	Impatient	Insecure	Nervous
Threatened	Wishy-Washy		

When you use these poor information sources for making your decisions, you may often find yourself standing at the Y in the road where your decisions take on the characteristics of being manipulative, unconscious, habitual, forced, quick, pressured, not weighed, and without counsel. If so, you may be feeling lost. You may find yourself realizing that the place where you ended up—the proverbial end of the road—was the lonely yet logical result of the selections that you made based on lies, confusion, a lack of purpose, depression, secrets, a lack of love, instability, or lack of fulfillment.

So let us review once again:

Your decisions are only as good as the information you use to make those decisions. Getting to good information—or better said, the truth—is the only foundation to good decision-making.

We have just learned that using the majority, the past, or our own feelings as information sources often do not give us the truth or provide much light, which means we are making *decisions in the dark*.

TRUTH AFFECTS DECISIONS

What if I told you that most of the answers to all of your leadership challenges are sitting in the same gap where you are standing. They are so close to you, even within an arm's length. Why then, if all of your answers are so close by, can you not see them? It is because without the truth, it is too dark to see those answers.

Any attempt to lead a situation to a better place—whether it is your own family, your business, or a personal challenge—is a waste of time unless you illuminate the gap with truth. Sure, you may enjoy some small and temporary victories without truth, but it takes truth to make a significant long-term impact.

Whatever gap you are standing in right now, do you feel like you are working in the dark?

How are the people around you feeling?

Are their minds clear as to where you are all going?

Do they know what behaviors they must change to do their part?

Do they know what their strengths and weaknesses are?

Are they feeling empowered to make decisions?

Do they know that it is OK to make mistakes?

What is their greatest fear right now?

If they could change one thing, what would it be?

Would it be something they would start doing, or something they would stop doing?

Do they really feel like part of the solution? Do their opinions really count?

Can you see clearly the mental *movie* of your vision of that better place? If you can, can you articulate it in such a way that the people around you can see the same movie?

Do you know how to get there?

Are you having success piecing together the puzzle, making the right decisions, the right moves, and the right conversations?

Unless the truth is illuminating the gap in which you are standing, you will never know the answers to these questions. You will find yourself in a situation similar to the jigsaw puzzle story we read earlier.

On the other hand, if you are able to make decisions in the light of truth, then you will be much more effective. The truth, once spoken and acted upon, will move situations forward effectively and quickly. The truth will take a situation that has been stagnant or spinning in circles for years and quickly get that situation back on track and moving to its *purposed* place.

If the truth needs to be our information source instead of sources like the majority, the past and our feelings, then what is the *truth*?

Do you believe there is such a thing as *truth*?

Truth about the universe?

Truth about a higher power?

Truth about life after death?

Truth about your life? Your marriage? Your kids? Your job?

I have found that there seems to be two categories we typically use when discussing truth as an information source:

1. Principle truths as an information source
2. People's truths as an information source

PRINCIPLE TRUTHS AS AN INFORMATION SOURCE

Principle truths include *love, honesty, integrity, respect, trust*, and *fairness*. These truths are self-evident and need no help from us. These truths have been at work for all time. They were not put into place by any woman or any man. Like with nature or the human body, it does not take much research to conclude that there must be an ultimate source of all truth. There are truths about how the human body and nature function that we cannot debate. Principle truths are very similar and just as unarguable. These principles are at work in our lives every day. The whole world could shake, but these truths do not change.

People may decide not to follow these truths, but that does not change the very fact of their existence. If you were to consider trying to build a business, a family, or a church on the opposites of these principle truths, then you would quickly see how self-evident they are. These invisible, principle truths that I just mentioned are similar to the truth of gravity. Gravity does not need our help to convince anyone of its realness and its power. Though invisible in nature, gravity scores a 100 percent confidence rating when I ask students how sure they are that my pen will drop to the floor once I release it. I then respond to my students, "If we are 100 percent confident that gravity rules the physical universe though it is not man-made and it is invisible, are we equally confident that these principle truths rule the interpersonal universe also being not man-made and being invisible in nature?" However, as much as we would all agree that we must align ourselves with the principle truths such as honesty and fairness, we often do not base our decisions on these unarguable truths. To make decisions based on these truths is to anchor yourself, the people you are leading, and your situation to an unchangeable, unmovable, and unshakeable foundation regardless of the environment.

When you base decisions on principle truths, you align yourself with powers on a higher plane. These powers run the interpersonal universe. When you anchor yourself and your decisions on these changeless principles, it is easier to deal with change. Principles do not need any defense. They defend themselves.

People's Truths as an Information Source

Let me refer you to a car accident witnessed from four different angles by four people. Each eyewitness has his or her own perspective regarding what happened and who was at fault, yet invariably those perspectives are all different. Each eyewitness believes that he or she is holding onto the truth while the others must either be giving false testimony or suffering from vision problems.

Do you believe there is an absolute truth for what happened in this accident? If so, then because of your humanity, you will likely never know exactly what that truth is.

Yet, to the degree we can compile the most truth about what happened in this accident, we still could most effectively and fairly settle the case. It would be as if we were operating on a scale of one to ten and if we could get as high as eight on the truth scale, then we also could get to an eight on the fairness scale.

People's truths define an event, a situation, someone's feelings, or perceptions. It is what we want from somebody when we say, "Tell me the truth." When we ask someone to tell the truth about how he or she feels, or what he or she perceives about something, or his or her opinion, or what it was he or she saw, we get *their individual* truth, which may or may not be actual truth. However, it is just as important as principle truth.

Imagine that you have just promoted an employee to a position handling much of the cash in your business. You just recently performed a wage review with this person and through a misunderstanding he perceives that you have gone back on your word to give him a raise. Even though what this employee perceives is not, in fact, true, how important do you believe it is that you should know what they believe to be true? Knowing what people believe to be true, whether it is the truth or not, can save a business, a family, a marriage, or even a church from self-destructing.

TRUTH TEARS DOWN AS WELL AS BUILDS UP

We said earlier that the truth, when brought into the open, progresses a situation to where it belongs. That may not necessarily be where we *want* it to go, or for that matter, the *way* in which we want it to get there. Truth makes a way where there appears to be no way.

Truth, by its very nature, will build up what needs building and tear down what needs destroying. Truth does the necessary work. The truth does not do the work incorrectly or to the wrong person. The truth does not play favorites. The truth knows no position. Whoever is delivering the truth at the time is the one with the authority. Truth will encourage or discipline, give wisdom or take away misunderstanding, reinforce direction or set new direction, convict or give peace. It will slam you against the wall and hold you accountable for your lies while on the very same day it will commend you for your compassion. *Sometimes the truth smacks us in the face and sometimes the truth pats us on the back.*

We must begin to see ourselves as leaders who serve up the truth with love. We do not do the work; the truth does the work. We must be facilitators of the truth. We do not satisfy the people's hunger; we just serve the food. We are like a waiter in a restaurant. When a waiter provides that service with love and kindness, how much better the experience is for everyone involved. On the other hand, if a waiter is disrespectful and difficult, the restaurant patrons may not even accept the food as served even though they know that it will satisfy their hunger. In the next lesson, we will address how *love* influences the gathering and distribution of truth.

How can the truth that is working in the gap be so powerful? How can it actually help us make progress toward the *better* situation?

Primarily, in two ways:

1. It *tears down* what is hindering progress
2. It *builds up* what is helping progress

And usually the truth does so in just that order. It is why you often hear the familiar saying; "Sometimes the situation must get worse before it gets better." As an example, I was asked to work with the Human Resources Department in our sister company, because it was experiencing a lot of confusion, and frustration, and, therefore, it was making very little progress. Knowing my decisions would only be as good as the information I used to make those decisions, I needed to get to the truth. As always I started out to perform the same three Life Leadership Lessons. I needed the truth primarily from the four key parties in this particular case and fortunately, I had developed caring relationships with all four of them. This was critical because unless my motives were clear (Lesson three), unless those four people knew that I truly cared for and wanted to help each one of them solve this problem, there would be very little chance that I would ever get to their truths (Lesson two).

They trusted me and understood that I had no other motives than to help their situation. I started by explaining that all of us would begin using the methodologies as contained in Life Leadership Lessons. We would start this process by gathering each person's truth about the current situation, the vision for a better situation that each person held, and then we could better determine the gap that divides the two (Lesson one).

I made it clear before we started that they must agree to tell nothing but the truth, no matter how ugly it may sound. I emphasized once again that they would need to realize that the truth takes things where they are supposed to go. This may not be the same place as where we desire them to go. This was a scary concept, but eventually they agreed to commit to the process because they realized, as we all need to realize, they needed to choose their pain; the pain of living in the truth or the pain of *not* living in the truth. They knew the pain of living *in* the truth is the only one that brings progress, and I think they had enough of the other pain and were ready to *get in the truth*, no matter how painful it would be.

I started my discussions with the Human Resources manager and a recruiter. Both of them vented much frustration as each shared their version of the current situation and the better place that each envisioned. After this truth session, we would take all the truth we were able to gather up to their supervisor, the Director of Human Resources. I wrote everything down, as I always do, so that when the four of us met if someone decided to chicken out and be unwilling to repeat everything to their supervisor that they had previously said only to me, I would then repeat it. This often happens especially when it's time to share harsh criticisms; that is when people start watering everything down and now it is no longer the truth. It is very important it stays word-for-word the way their original truth came out (of course, being respectful and not violating the principle truths).

When this happens, I make sure every truth is spoken even if I have to be the one to do it. I did warn them all in advance that I would be doing this if I believed it to be necessary. The director listened to their criticisms, and then began to share his truth. We discovered that he was similarly frustrated. After gathering all of that truth, we then went to see the president of the company and proceeded to share with him all the truths that we had gathered up to that point. We then asked him for his truth.

Wow! As he revealed the future vision (better situation) that he had of the Human Resources Department, I quickly saw that we were all heading for a "Duh!" moment. The lights went on simultaneously inside the heads of all involved. Issues that previously were muddy, suddenly became very clear. All of their frustrations about why certain requests were not making it to the top of the company's priority list suddenly made sense. Upon leaving that meeting, it also became perfectly clear that the Human Resource manager and the recruiter would soon be looking for new careers due to the misalignment of future visions.

The differences between their vision of the better situation and the president's vision were very different and likely never would be close. Within months, they both had moved on to new jobs. Today, they are both doing well because the truth put them where they should be, and it removed them from where they were. The truth worked because it moved round pegs to round holes. The truth moved them, maybe not to where they thought they were heading, but certainly it moved them to where they should be because the *truth works*. They went forward, and once they were gone, then the Human Resources Department could go forward as well, although in a much different direction than it was moving previously, in the direction that it was purposed to go.

WALLS HINDER PROGRESS

As a leader trying to move the people within your ten-foot circle to the *better* place, what typically holds back your progress or prevents any movement?

Walls.

Walls stop or slow progress. Therefore, tearing down walls or barriers usually starts or increases the pace toward progress. These walls have a goal. Their goal is to divide, separate, and isolate people. If that is accomplished, then businesses, families and churches will divide, fall, and make no progress in closing the gap and moving toward the promised land of *better*. If you can keep people apart from each other, then they can live in the same house, work in the same business, or go to the same church but still make little or no progress toward *better*. If there is a wall between you and me, then we cannot unite. If we cannot unite, we cannot make progress.

Some of these walls are:

Walls of lies and deception
Walls of pride and ego
Walls of indecision
Walls of unclear expectations (I like to call these jump balls.)
Walls of no vision of the better place
Walls of no knowledge of unmet needs, pains and hurts
Walls of resentment
Walls of jealousy
Walls of no forgiveness
Walls of bitterness
Walls of anger
Walls of frustration
Walls of confusion and misunderstandings
Walls of distortions and exaggerations

You will notice that most of these walls are walls of emotion or feelings. We may have walls of emotion that link us to a particular person or situation. Every time we are near that person or in that situation, then these walls come up to keep the situation stagnant. The presence of emotion shows us that there is a problem present that we must solve. Emotions do not show us how to solve the problem. Emotions are like smoke. The smoke tells us that there is a fire, but the smoke does not tell us what caused the fire, or even how to put the fire out. However, the smoke is truth and so are the emotions.

Speaking the truth in love can take down any one of these walls even if it took us ten years or more to build up and reinforce those walls. Sometimes it takes a season of time to do all of this. At other times, the truth can tear down those same walls in the blink of an eye. When the truth tears down one of these walls in you, it can literally buckle you over a chair, cause your face to cringe, make you feel as if you have gone stone dead while still standing with your eyes open, stop you from eating for days, cause sleepless nights, or cause you to stay in bed for a week. I believe there are people today who are in hospitals or who are taking medication after a diagnosis of all manner of depression when they are simply suffering from an exposure to *truth*.

Whatever you do, do not run away. Let *truth* do its work in you and accomplish the tearing down and building up process. Truth will do the work that is necessary, and it will bring progress. If you run away from truth, or search for ways to numb the pain of those crumbling walls, all you are going to do is prolong and delay the pain that you must eventually suffer. You may well turn a one-year lesson into a five-year lesson. Don't do it!

Just the other day one of my subordinates shared with me that certain employees find my methods to be intimidating. I was thrilled that someone was actually giving me this type of truthful feedback.

I asked my subordinate to help me better understand why others thought that I was intimidating. He really struggled, so I tried to help.

"Is it that I yell?" I asked him.

"No," he replied.

"Is it that I threaten?"

Again, he responded in the negative.

"Help me out then," I said.

"Larry, I think people are intimidated because once you get on to something, you don't get off of it until you get to the truth of the matter," was his reply.

"So, I intimidate them by the *way* I do that?" I asked.

"No, I guess it is the *truth that you might find,* that they are afraid of," he said.

"Then they should be afraid!" was my response.

It is productive to be afraid of the truth.

It is not productive to be afraid of a person.

TRUTH BUILDS UP WHAT IS HELPING PROGRESS

We have already discussed that the truth is what helps progress, so whatever truth is currently at the surface of a situation will reinforce or build up more truth. Remember, I said that the truth defends itself. Well, it also builds itself up.

Wherever there is the practice of principle truths—by this, I mean a practice of love, honesty, integrity, respect, trust, and fairness—there you will find people's truth, and thus you will also find light. One drives the other. Truth builds on itself and supports itself in much the same way that when we find ourselves in a darkened room, we may use a flashlight to find the light switch.

Truth also grows people and situations upward and forward to the places that they rightfully belong.

ACTIVITY PAGE FOR LESSON TWO

Go back to page 33 and review the three worlds and nine specific areas that you must lead. Consider what information sources you have mostly used to make decisions in each area. Have you mostly used Bad Information Sources (be sure to review the feelings that you circled earlier) or Truth Information Sources? Based on your reflection, place each one of the nine areas under one of the two categories below.

Bad Information Sources: Majority, Past, and Feelings:

_____

_____

_____

Truth Information Sources: Principle Truths, and People's Truths:

_____

_____

_____

Lesson 3

MOTIVES OF LOVE CREATE AN ENVIRONMENT OF TRUTH

Motives of Love

We have learned that the most powerful thing we can do to close the gap between our current situation and a desired better situation is to fill the gap with truth. We want to inject it, pack it, and saturate it with truth. The truth will tear down what is hindering progress and build up what is helping progress. It will move you and those you are leading closer to the *better* place. However, truth cannot do anything until you deliver it. You might have access to a truck full of food with which to feed hungry and dying people, but unless you deliver that food, there will be no healing, progress, or victory over hunger. You have access to your own principle truths and personal truths, but unless you deliver them, you will stay right where you are in the current situation.

To hold back the truth is to hold back progress. To say this in another way, the degree to which you are *not in the truth* about a particular situation is the same degree to which you will struggle with that situation.

We must now talk about *how* we fill the gap with truth.

Our hearts conceive the truth and our mouths deliver it, but most people do not speak the truth. What is the biggest problem in speaking truth? Is it that we do not have the truth in our hearts to deliver? Is it that we have truth in our hearts but we will not let it come out of our mouths? My experience has been that 80 percent of the time our principle and personal truths are clear in our hearts, but we will not let them out of our mouths. Why?

Because of fear.

FEAR IS THE ENEMY OF LOVE AND TRUTH

Consider this scenario: A new leader comes on board and his task is to turn around a problem location so that it begins to make a profit. Very quickly, the new leader decides that he must talk to the people involved in the situation and find out what problems are occurring so that he can fix those problems. He concludes this will be an easy task. The leader talks to everybody, gathers much information, and makes some business decisions based on what the people tell him. The leader implements an action plan. These strategies are well organized, have several methodical steps, and even utilize state of the art technology. The plan executes right on schedule, but it does not work. The leader cannot figure out what went wrong with his action plan.

The problem is the leader never stopped to consider that the information he or she gathered from the new employees may have been anything other than the truth. It is probably not so much a case that the employees lied to the leader, but rather a case where their information was selective, distorted, and incomplete. After all, the people providing the information were likely thinking one or all of the following questions. Who is this new leader? What are his or her motives? Which of our routines will the leader change? Will he or she take offense to my feedback? Thus, the new leader received feedback that was motivated by fear. The leader then made business decisions based on that bad information, and that is why the leader ended up with bad results.

The fact remains: Our decisions are only as good as the information we use to make those decisions.

Fear = false/distorted information = bad decisions = bad results

Love/trust = truth/accurate information = good decisions = good results

We now know that to hold back truth is to hold back progress. The single most common thing that holds back truth is *fear*.

FEAR OF PAIN

Where there is fear, there lie hidden truths or captive truths that must be set free so you can add these truths to your pool of information from which you will make good decisions. Where there is fear, there cannot be effective decision making. Fear can cause us to suppress the truth. It is not natural for truth to be suppressed, so when we suppress truth out of fear we are fighting a principle. We learned earlier that one never wins by fighting against a principle. Suppressed truth can cause high blood pressure, heart attacks, and all manner of stress-related illnesses. As well, the truth released can cause a release of stress and better health.

Let us look at some of the more common fears of pain:

Fear of confrontation
Fear of embarrassment
Fear of failure
Fear of being found out
Fear of being rejected
Fear of having your feelings hurt
Fear of loss of security (job)
Fear of poor reputation
Fear of finding out that the truth is not what you thought or wanted

Below is a short story in a business setting of how the truth and love overcomes fear and moves a situation forward.

Joe, a team leader at a small factory, is very frustrated with his manager, Bob. Bob has recently been very preoccupied and absent-minded which is causing huge problems in work flowing smoothly through the factory. Joe is at the end of his emotional rope, especially because the company bases his pay on the rate of production and Bob's preoccupation has caused Joe's pay to drop in each of the last several months. As well, Joe knows that his fellow team members are also upset. The pressure on Joe is mounting from all sides.

Joe assumes Bob no longer cares about the work place. The truth is, Bob is going through some marriage problems and does not want anyone to know. Bob fears embarrassment. He knows his lack of attention to the business is causing problems for the people around him, and he also is aware that

Joe—normally a caring and cooperative worker—is now cold and short-tempered with him.

As part of an annual development program, Bob and Joe attend a one-day Life Leadership Lessons session. After a couple of days pondering their newfound insights, Joe realizes he is letting the *fear of confrontation* hold him back from speaking truth to Bob about his absent-mindedness. Joe realizes that if he is to truly be a leader, he must influence those within his ten-foot circle. This means that the truth starts with him. Joe finally confronts Bob, his manager, and tells him everything that is in his heart. Meanwhile, Bob also realizes that he has allowed the *fear of embarrassment* to hold him back from being truthful about his marriage problems. He also concludes correctly that if a leader is to influence those within his or her ten-foot circle, then the circle of truth must start with him.

Bob tells Joe about the personal situation at home and how it is affecting him at work. Moved by compassion, Joe immediately drops his frustration toward Bob and instead shows Bob patience and understanding. Thus, the current situation moves closer to the better situation as the result of conquering fear and broadcasting truth.

Joe realizes that the truth he once held about Bob not seeming to care for the factory any more was not actually a truth at all. Joe further considers his motives through all of this (Lesson three). He realizes his motives were more about fixing his own pay, than caring for Bob and if he had put Bob first he would have spoken the truth in love much earlier with Bob and avoided most of the production problems. He realizes that Bob is a real guy with real problems just like him. He realizes Bob trusted him enough to share something personal. Joe and Bob decide that they must talk to all the other people and inject more truth into the gap. They do so, and as a team, the entire work force comes up with a plan to step up production and support Bob during his personal crisis. They even take responsibility for a portion of Bob's workload until Bob gets through this challenging season.

Does this next short story in a church setting sound familiar to you?

In a well-intentioned, local church on Sunday, the people show up and greet one another. They respond to one another's greeting by stating they are doing great and God is blessing them. In truth, many of them have teenagers struggling with drugs and there has been a recent increase in drug dealer activity in their city. However, out of fear of embarrassment (or poor reputation) they hold those truths. During church they take a vote and conclude that the church should go forward and invest time and money in the new "furniture ministry" to provide poor people with better furniture. The problem is, they are fixing the wrong problem (or one of lesser priority) and most people know it, but will not say anything. Until truth is spoken, this current situation will not move to the better situation. Your decisions are only as good as the information you use to make them. They made this decision on bad information.

How do we overcome this fear of pain? Well, if you understand that to *not* live truthfully is the same as trying to outwit the truth and that you *will* eventually lose, then you will also understand that this is a matter of choosing your pain. It can be painful to live in the truth, but it is *more* painful not to do so. The leader who ignores the principle of truth and assumes that this will help him or her to avoid pain is as foolish as a man who jumps off a high-rise building ignoring the principle of gravity. The principle will win. When I realize that someone fears the truth, I usually say to that person, "Be afraid! However, don't let that fear stop you from acting on the truth!"

To be afraid of the truth is OK. To be afraid of a person is not OK. That kind of fear will never lead to lasting progress.

Remember also that the truth always wins. We must respect the truth, submit to the truth, and ultimately commit to the truth.

FILLING THE GAP WITH THE LIGHT OF TRUTH

The light of truth illuminates and eliminates. It illuminates what is real and eliminates what is false. It builds up what is real and tears down what is false.

If truth is light and we do not want to be in the dark, how do we fill the gap with truth so we stay in the light?

START WITH YOURSELF
IN YOUR TWO-FOOT CIRCLE OF TRUTH

First, let us get one thing clear. You are the biggest obstacle to getting into the truth.

You cannot illuminate your ten-foot circle with truths that you have not allowed to come into your own two-foot circle. When I say *two-foot circle*, I mean in your own head, in your own heart. That is where the lights of truth have to come on first, before you can speak that truth, that light, into your ten-foot circle where it will help all of those around you. You may have to meditate and talk to yourself a little bit. Work out the truth with yourself first.

As an example, a supervisor where I work will often come to me for help. This is how a typical conversation usually develops.

"Larry, you have to help me," a supervisor will say to me. "I have a manager that I just can't get to move."

Using my knowledge of the model for leading in the gap, I ask, "What is the *better* situation that you are trying to move that manager toward?"

At this point, the supervisor usually buries his head in his hands and says, "You always do this to me."

He does not know the answer to that question because he never took the time to get clear in his own head, to illuminate his two-foot circle with the truth of the better situation that he wanted this person to get to. How is he to get this manager to the better situation when he cannot even tell me where that is? At this point, I usually tell the supervisor that he must take some quiet time and get his 2ft circle illuminated with the truth about the manager's current situation and vision of a better situation. Then he needs to go share that truth with the manager and see if they even agree on those two steps. If so, together they should compile the three actions steps to close the gap, which should be kind of a "Duh" process once the current situation and better situation is clear.

I know that the one thing that will most likely distort truth more than anything else is me. I have had many, many experiences of seeking truth only to find out that the truth was not what I was sure it was.

I recently was going out to one of our sites to help with a personnel problem. The site had approximately eight employees and was having problems for a long time and those problems had escalated dramatically. At the time, I was training the new Human Resources Manager (who was not in the division I work for but I was asked to help) and I decided to bring her along thinking she could benefit from the experience. On our way to the location, she asked me–somewhat concerned–what we were going to do to fix the situation. I responded that I did not yet know, and I would not know until I had discovered what it was that the truth would tell me to do. The best chance I had to discern the truth was to keep my thinking in a neutral position and refrain from any attempt to preconceive what I thought the truth might be. I know that I am the greatest risk to introducing falsehood into a situation.

Start with yourself. Whatever size gap you may be standing in right now, you cannot make an impact on the people in your 10-foot circle until you make that same impact on your two-foot circle. The first step involves delving into the truth. Draw a two-foot circle on the ground and step into the center of it. Then start to fill that area with truth. As a leader, you will be able to reach and teach those you are leading on how to live truthfully. The most powerful method of influence is by example. Creating an environment of truth starts with you. You must be committed to walking truthfully before you will ever influence anyone else to walk truthfully. You must be more committed to the truth than you are to *being right*.

So let us start with an honest look at your current situation. Are the people who surround you walking in the truth? Are they being transparent by saying what is on their minds with no fear? Do you notice that the people around you usually do not *open up* when they are in your presence? Perhaps the truth eventually will get to you, but by then the truth is always relayed via a third party? Do you feel that sometimes you are the *last to know*? Do your meetings tend to be very quiet? Do the people around you simply look at each other and wait for someone else to start talking? When you sit down with a family member or with an employee, do you notice that things get so quiet that you find yourself doing all the talking?

Before you start pointing fingers at everyone else, I am going to suggest that you are the truth problem. Remember, we are working on the two-foot circle right now—just on you.

Why would people not feel comfortable to be completely honest when they come into your ten-foot circle? Does it feel warm and safe in there? Is it scary, risky and unpredictable? Do you later discover that people told you what they thought you wanted to hear instead of telling you the truth? If they are doing that, then you are getting a lot of bad information that you are probably using to base your decisions.

If some of these problems sound familiar, I think we should talk about motives.

Often, people go into leadership roles for the wrong reason. Especially in business, but not necessarily limited to that endeavor, people usually go into the leadership role for selfish reasons. These reasons include the need to feel important, to feel worthy, to feel significant, to gain recognition, to exercise power and control, or simply to make more money. The leadership role, by nature, tempts and draws in the average person who feels a lack of significance or contentment in his or her life and thinks being a leader will bring personal fulfillment. Unconsciously or consciously, these people invariably believe that the leadership role will make them whole and content. What a formula for disaster—a guaranteed and almost programmed course toward failure. Why? Because the character qualities and types of behavior that one must exercise in order to ensure that a leader has power, control, and recognition are, by nature, the exact opposites of the qualities needed by that same person in order to effectively lead others.

Effective leadership—truly serving others—always requires the leader to regularly put him or herself into painful situations in order to maintain a culture of truth. If your reasons for going into leadership are self-serving, you will never discipline yourself to perform these acts of self-sacrifice. In fact, the pain of leadership will quickly drown out any dreams you may have of fame, money, or control. You will bail out. People who are in the leadership role for the wrong reasons often reveal later that the leadership challenge is a stressful burden instead of an exciting challenge.

I was once doing some Life Leadership Lesson training with a manager. During the course of our sessions, I often would ask him, "How did you love your people today?" I asked precisely this question because this is the foundation upon which everything else builds.

This question would always frustrate the manager. I would then discuss how he must both talk and walk out his motives of love by finding and celebrating victories, encouraging others, patting people on the back, sincerely checking in with people to make sure they were OK, casting his better vision of them , etc.

Then, one day when I asked the question, "How did you love your people?" he finally came out with the truth and abruptly said, "You don't pay me enough to do that!"

Wow! The lights went on and that truth cleared everything up.

"You're right!" I said. "I could never pay you enough to do that. You must volunteer that part on your own. Until you can do that, the victories you so much desire in leadership will never occur."

If you choose a leadership role because you love people and want to make a difference in people's lives, you will persevere. In fact, regardless of your title, position, or authority, you will find a way to make that difference.

Let us look at the word *motive*. First, when I ask most people what they think of when I say the word *motives*, as in "This person has motives," they attach it to something bad. Of course, a motive can be either good or bad.

The definition of motive is: something as a reason or desire acting as a spur to action; or something causing or capable of causing motion. Now, look at the word *motivated*, which comes from motive.

A person is motivated by his or her motive. When someone is motivated by motives of love, you cannot stop them. They have an endless reservoir of energy, power and drive. Like Martin Luther King Jr. who was motivated by love, only a bullet could stop him and yet today his message is alive and still making a difference.

Based on a true story, *Cinderella Man* is a movie about a retired, busted up ex-boxer who has to go back to the ring during the Depression just to feed his children. Wanting only to earn money for his family—even if it meant getting regularly beat up in the ring—this boxer ends up becoming the heavy-weight world champion. What did he have over the other boxers? He was motivated by love for his children. At a celebration press conference the reporters asked this boxer just what made him tick; what drove him to do such an amazing thing and he responded by saying, "Milk." You cannot stop someone motivated by love.

So why exactly did you take this leadership role? What is the point? Is this about paying the bills, or is it more than that? Is this about fulfilling what your parents wanted you to do? What is your goal, the real goal, the one you do not tell anyone else? Is it even *your* goal? Is your *heart* in it? Is it a spouse's goal? A boss's goal and maybe you do not agree with that goal?

To truly illuminate your two-foot circle, you may need time for prayer and meditation to listen to your own heart's desire, your own thoughts, or your own self-talk. What are you saying to yourself? Is it the truth? What are your motives to do the things you do? You must s-l-o-w d—o—w—n long enough to hear your own thoughts and be able to seek your own motives. You must then take note of the feelings that will surface within you. Where are you following feelings instead of truth? Do you remember the example of those splits in the roads that we must select? Sometimes we are moving so rapidly down life's highway that we pass alternate routes without even realizing it.

When a leader has motives other than love, everyone else usually knows before the leader. The leader is usually the last person to find out, and that is because it usually dawns on him only when everyone he is attempting to lead decides to quit following.

What is in our hearts—motives—comes out of our mouths loud and clear. If our motive is anything other than helping people through care and love, the people around us will know it. We must each search our hearts and detect what it wants, because our heart desires, our motives project like movies to the people we are leading. Our motives show up on our faces, in our words, our body language, our tone of voice, and in our vocal inflections. If you are struggling to create an environment where people can speak the truth, hear the truth, and act upon the truth, then look into your own heart to find the problem. Out of the abundance of the heart, the mouth speaks. No matter how hard you try, the motive of your heart will be revealed in what you say, how you say it, in the order you say it, in the tone you say it, in the words you select and the words you leave out, and even in your facial expressions that are unconsciously timed on certain words. You are a fool to think you can keep this hidden. The people around you already know. The loudest words heard whenever you speak are the words that you are not saying aloud.

Whether you use the words *love* and *care,* or whether you use the words *making a difference,* if your motive is to help people, then you will succeed. The principles of the universe are behind you to make sure that happens. However, you must never forget that *love*—one of those principle truths we mentioned earlier—is a *verb.*

THE POWER OF LOVE

Love, if applied, is the most powerful force in the universe.

Love has the power to…open mouths to speak the truth.

Love has the power to…open ears to hear the truth.

Love has the power to…open minds to learn new truths.

Love has the power to…stop people from running away from painful truths even as the walls of division are being torn down around them.

Love has the power to…give all of life purpose.

Love prevents people from being victims. How can someone who loves me make me a victim? On the other hand, consider a young child who always sees him or herself as victimized by parents. These individuals always have an excuse ready and nothing is ever his or her fault. Lacking the understanding of love, they default to their basic nature. Yet, as a child grows to an adult and learns about love, he or she will often reflect and say, "Now I realize it was because my parents loved me that they did this, or would not let me do that."

As long as a person *thinks* there is some underlying selfish motive as to why you are sharing truths, he will not hear the truth. He will be unable to repeat what you said even one day later. At best, he will hear the words, but surely, will not accept them as truth. Neither will he take any action based on words he does not believe are truth. From these individuals, there is no desire to understand, to learn, to be accountable, or to change behavior. They will continue to take on the role of a victim because that is what releases them of any responsibility. When a person knows that you truly care about him—in fact, love them—that is when you truly remove all his thoughts of being a victim. That is when he knows you are sharing this truth because you want to help him. Now, there is a desire to understand, to learn. He allows himself to be accountable, and then he wants to change his own behavior.

Love is the glue that keeps people's feet glued to the floor and stops them from running while hearing painful truths. Never assume people already know that you love them and care about them. Restate that you care, especially before having the tough truth conversations.

CASTING A BETTER VISION

I have an exercise that I often do at the end of my classes. I pair each person with a partner, and then I ask them to hug, as a way to show motives. Then, I ask each partner in each pair to tell the other person the better situation or vision that he or she has for the other. They do this simply by saying, "I believe in you and I know you are going to improve after going to this class." Or we say things that start with, "Imagine this.." or, "Let's talk about the next level…" This usually is a very powerful exercise, and it only takes about fifteen seconds. I also share with the class that if you cannot give someone a hug and encourage them, get the heck out of leadership! If you plan on influencing people to get to the better situation, if you want to tap the hidden 30 percent potential, you must believe it (the better situation) before you ever see it, if you want to receive it.

Always remember…"Love them before you lead them."

I was training a new district manager and we were out in the field visiting sites. At the end of the day I asked him what he learned. He said, "Awhile ago I learned that I must have the vision of the better situation for these sites if I'm to help them get there. But today watching you interact with the people, you carry a vision of the better situation not only for the site, but more importantly for each person. For example, when we met Bill you cast your better vision of Bill so as Bill heard you articulate it he could begin to see himself at a higher level. I could see it was encouraging and lifting up while at the same time convicting him of his current poor performance. But when you were done he was mad at himself, not you."

However, love has no power to do anything unless you activate the power of love, which means that you must then *act in love,* as love is a verb.

Do you really want to change the world—your ten-foot world—and make a difference? Do you now understand that you cannot beat the truth and that the truth always wins? Do you fully realize that you and you alone must choose your pain?

Are you ready to jump in to leadership? Are you willing to speak the truth? Are you willing to hear the truth? Do you have truths that you have been holding back for years and years? It is always easier to share truths that put others at risk. Are you willing to voice those truths that put *you* at risk? Are you willing to inflict pain on yourself in order to gain wisdom, truth, knowledge, and fulfillment? Are you willing to daily walk and speak the truth about the gap between your current situation and the better situation? Are you willing to start casting your vision of *better* every day so that people around you can no longer ignore the gap?

Shining the light of truth into the gap where you stand is up to you!

Are you ready to start with you? Are you willing to go to the next board meeting and say what you are really thinking? Are you ready to go to dinner with your spouse and say what you have been thinking but have been afraid to say for several months or maybe even years?

Exposing your insides to others is a scary process, but it must start with the leader. Are you ready to take the consequences? Remember, you are speaking your truths, but they may or may not be *the* truth.

If you believe that truth is light and that turning on the lights must start with you, I know that you will do all of this and more. By doing so, you will begin a process of *truth telling*—or truth boxing, which we will discuss later—that will move your situation forward. It may not be pretty at first, but as we said earlier, the truth usually tears down what is false first before it builds up what is true.

Remember, as you share your own truths with others, they may begin to share their truths with you. Also, remember that sharing each other's truths will begin to clean out what is false on both sides. This cleansing process will begin to make things clear. The process of making decisions—both small and big—will begin to improve for everyone because everyone will be basing his or her own decisions on a greater portion of truth.

For example, let us imagine a situation where I, a fellow employee, come out and finally share a truth of mine that I believe you have been angry with me because I received that promotion last month that you thought you were entitled. In turn, you respond with your truth by saying, "Well, that is only half true."

You confirm that you have been angry with me, but your anger is not about the promotion because you truly thought I was the best person for the job. Instead, you have been angry that ever since I have taken on the new position, I have not been relying on your judgment and providing you with a role as my right-hand man. That is what you expected I would do. Instead, you were disappointed that I was using you less and backing away from you even more.

I agree with you. I then share that I was doing so only because I thought you were upset about not landing the promotion.

Wow, we both agree! This sharing of truths totally changes things! You want to lock arms with me and I with you. This wall of misunderstanding was keeping us away from each other. The truth tears down the walls and will allow unity and teamwork to build. The results will be quick and substantial. The situation will quickly begin to move forward to the place of *better*.

Note that the tool is the mouth. Our mouth is a very, very sharp tool much as a razor-sharp knife in the hands of a surgeon with a motive to heal can save a patient's life. Yet, the same tool wielded by a thug with a motive to kill will most likely take a life. The same tool used with different motives produces two very different outcomes.

In my life, I have discovered people who could take truth and use it in very destructive ways. Gossip, for example, may take what is truth and deliver it to the wrong person. This will invariably move a situation backward instead of forward.

Truth telling is a responsibility that we all must take seriously. There is a truth about how responsible adults make babies, but we do not tell that truth to a five-year-old child. If love is your motive, it will guide you through every situation of truth-telling to be sure that you handle your mouth—this very sharp tool—in the most productive way.

Maybe you do fairly well at walking in the truth and speaking truthfully, but it is the *way* that you speak that leaves you as the only one who is speaking the truth. What I mean by this is that the people around you may know that you are a person who will say what is on your mind. They know exactly where you stand on an issue, but they will never speak so candidly in return. Why is it that when you share your truths, you are pushing away others from sharing their truths? It is probably because your heart is spilling out in your words, and they know it even if you do not. If you overreact, become disrespectful, insult others, talk down to them, or mock anyone in the way as you share your truth, people will shut down sharing their truths. You will never get truth from them in return. This will leave you in the dark. Eventually, you will lose.

If this sounds familiar, check your true motives. If your heart is critical, judgmental, biased, or seeking its own selfish end, then your words will reflect it. If your motive is not love but instead to just succeed and get ahead, then the people around you will become mere tools for your use. When the tools no longer work, your frustration will play like a movie on your face and reveal whom it is you are really serving—yourself. Just because you are being truthful does not mean everyone else will be truthful. This is the typical problem of trying to create truth in the ten-foot circle when you lack so much truth about your own motives in the two-foot circle.

The eye cannot see the eye. Having self-awareness—seeing our true self—is difficult. It usually takes another person to help us truly see ourselves. That is why it is so important to get counsel from people whom you trust to help you stay in the truth. You should always be seeking out the truth about yourself from those you lead.

I regularly do formal and informal reverse appraisals. I ask others for three things that they believe I do well. I also ask them to describe three things that they believe I should improve. I do this because I am the leader. I am the one who needs to facilitate and lead them into this environment of truth. I can only do this by and through example. I can attract truth only by showing that I am caring, loving, compassionate, understanding, humble, and have empathy as well as the ability to simply listen.

On the other hand, what if it is the people you lead that are sharing truths in inappropriate ways. Often, when you finally get a person who has not shared truth in a long time to share his or her truth, the words all come tumbling out with great emotion. This may include a lot of anger and even some poor choices of words. Remember this: Out of the mouth spills the heart. You may have just glimpsed deeply into this person's heart. The experience may leave you in shock or disappointment. Based on what we have just discussed, if you overreact to this sharing of truth, you might shut that person back down. They might say, "See, I finally shared the truth like you asked me to do and all it did was get me in trouble."

The key here is to praise the courage that person took to be honest with you, and then only later address the issues of heart and style. At these times focus in on the message and ignore the messenger's style. These are good problems to have because they are signs you are on your way to creating a culture of truth.

GET OTHERS TO JOIN YOU IN THE TRUTH

Even if you do all the right things, society is programming other people not to share their truths. In most cases, if someone openly admits the truth about his own weaknesses, fears, or mistakes at the office, someone may use these truths against him instead of using them to teach the person. Certainly, few will commend someone on their commitment and courage to speak the truth. Most organizations are not committed to creating a culture of truth. Therefore, they do not look for or commend behaviors that genuinely show a commitment to the truth.

Before we discuss getting others into the truth or creating an environment of truth, let us discuss the sport of boxing as an analogy to speaking the truth. I like the principles involved in the sport of boxing. The sport is straightforward. A boxer knows that it is the other guy's intention to knock him or her out, and the opponent knows that is also your intention. There are no hidden motives. Each boxer is motivated to connect. You do not get into a boxing ring and then question why you are there. They do not deceive the other boxer as to the reasons for their appearance in the ring. Each boxer delivers his or her intentions with both fists and tries to connect with the opponent. When a boxer is successful, everyone knows it.

Delivering truth should be that obvious. Instead, we sugarcoat our truths; we throw subtle hints, and we even send subliminal messages. However, none of these methods ever work. We even convince ourselves we were truthful. We say things like, "Boy, I sure was blunt with him. I just gave him a piece of my mind and what you see is what you get."

If you really want to know how clearly you communicate, try this test for one week. Every time you finish communicating something, ask the person to repeat back to you what it was he heard and what it is he is to learn or do based on the conversation.

I wager that what you hear will shock you. Like boxing, we must make leadership a contact sport. We need to connect like boxers do, but we cannot do that unless truths are surfaced for both parties. Both parties must see the lights come on and *bam*, there is a connection.

To really help someone, you must communicate in a manner that works for that person. You must know *where he or she is coming from.* Once you know from what point of reference he is coming, then you can go meet him there and make a connection. You must go to his neighborhood and talk to him there. You need to meet him where he is, *wherever* that is.

If you want to help an elderly woman cross the street, you do not stand on one side of the road and yell to her to cross over. You go across the road to meet her. You go to where *she is* and that is where you connect with her. You take hold of her hand and you help her to the other side of the street. We always want to help people from *our* own neighborhood because that is where things are most familiar and comfortable for us. We know what we mean. It is easier to use our wording, our habits of communication, our slang, our examples, and our stories. We assume that everyone else will know what all these things mean. After all, everyone in my neighborhood knows what I mean.

Sometimes we extend our hand to meet someone where he is but he will not give us his hand. This means that he is not yet willing or ready to get into the truth for various reasons. As a leader, you must continue to love this person even as you move on to the next person who truly wants your help. That is only fair.

To better understand ourselves and those we are leading, let us look at the four typical behavioral types in light of our teaching:

Passive-Everyone's truths matter except for theirs. They think, "Everyone else is the king of my kingdom".

Aggressive-Reveals perceived truths with such force as to create fear so that no one will ever challenge them. They are the kings of their kingdoms as long as they have instilled enough fear that no one challenges their perceived truths. To have one of their truths challenged and proven wrong is to lose their crown.

Passive Aggressive-Will not reveal perceived truths so they are not challenged and potentially proven false or partially false. They are the kings of their kingdoms as long as they keep it a private club.

Assertive-Everyone's truth matters including his or her truth. Principle (God's) truth is king of everyone's kingdom.

However, with tremendous patience we must seek the truth with the purpose of finding it. We must diligently seek, search, probe, dig, discover, and uncover with endless perseverance even as we would search for gold or silver. Just as a crazy gold miner will never give up, we must listen, ask, dig, dig some more, and never give up until we understand.

VAGUE GENERALITIES HURT THE TRUTH

Most people speak in vague generalities. As our society becomes increasingly fast-paced, we spend more and more time on the surface of life. We no longer have the time to get to the truth. It is common to pass somebody in the office hallway and speak in vague generalities:

"Hi, how is the project going?"

"Fine. How about you? How are you doing?"

"Fine."

When in truth, the project is at a standstill and my teenager is on drugs.

Vague generalities have now made their way into staff meetings, Friday night dates with our spouse, that special time with our kids, etc.

Vague generalities are a leader's worst enemy. As a leader, do not accept them or give them. Stop vague generalities in their tracks. When someone gives you one, ask another question. Ask why. Ask why again, and then ask why one more time. Force the practitioners of vague generalities to produce for you a movie frame by frame so you can see exactly what it is that they are saying. If they skip a frame, make them go back over the same topic until the movie is complete. Gain a full understanding of the topic of their speech.

When speaking, speak as if you are producing a movie, frame by frame. Have a beginning and an end to whatever you say. Keep your words clear, concise, and in order.

Seek truth. Keep repeating back whatever someone has told you until the other person acknowledges, "You have it!"

Love will cause you to develop excellent communication skills. Seek the truth with all your might. Ask questions. Do not lead people with your words, tone, or body language. We say, "I think this is a great idea. What do you think?" And then we wonder why we remain in the dark. Ask *why* until you get to the truth. Probe and look for underlying beliefs that drive another person's thoughts and words. Listen with your whole self, not just with your ears.

If you are able to do this day in and day out, eventually you will do this without even thinking about it. It will become a habit of interaction and the process you use to make decisions.

Seeking, finding, and acting on the truth could improve your life and the lives of those you are leading. It could even save your life here on earth and impact where you spend eternity.

If because you read this book you go and take just one action step that you would otherwise not have taken, it was worth my writing this book.

Do it.

Go share and exercise your motives of love (Lesson three), so your environment produces more truth and thus better decisions (Lesson two), so your gap closes and you move toward the better situation (Lesson one).

If you have just one victory from taking action, I want to hear about it. My contact information is on the back of the book. Call or e-mail me and let us celebrate that leadership victory together.

ACTIVITY PAGE FOR LESSON THREE

Fill out this model again and reflect on the differences as you compare it to the one you filled out after the first lesson. Consider the particular area that you are trying to make better and write down three things that best describe the current situation, three things that best describe the better situation, and three action steps that you have been considering to close the gap.

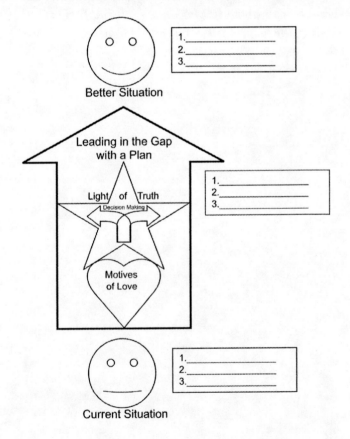

Better Situation

1._____
2._____
3._____

Leading in the Gap
with a Plan

Light of Truth

Decision Making

1._____
2._____
3._____

Motives
of Love

Current Situation

1._____
2._____
3._____

Final Thoughts on Taking Action

Nothing fails like success. Repeatedly I have seen leaders succeed for a day, week, or month and then revert to their old ways of behavior and the same struggles they thought they had left behind. Why is that? I think when the pain of our leadership struggle becomes greater than the pain of leaving our comfort zone, that is the moment we take action. Then, as we progress and the pain of the challenge subsides, we tend to want to shrink back into our old comfort zone. That is when we slip back into our old patterns of behavior. We must not try to finish our challenge using our old ways when our new way of truth and love is what got us out of the hole and onto the path to *better*. We must also be realistic that we cannot un-become in a week, or maybe even a month, what it took us thirty or forty years to become. However, we can make a difference if we are willing to exercise *daily discipline in a defined direction.*

I cannot stress enough all that you can learn simply by forcing yourself into leadership challenges where the only way out is to learn and learn quickly. I guess I subscribe to the method of learn-to-swim-by-getting-thrown-into-the-pool, or should I say throwing yourself into the pool. This forces us to learn from experience, and *there is a world of difference between learning something by reading it and learning something by bleeding it.* You simply must live certain things in order to understand them. Whether your leadership challenge is a teenager or a large corporation, start small with your two-foot circle. Do well with that little bit before you decide to tackle a larger task. Take steps of faith and follow your heart.

You know, I barely made it through high school. I never attended college, and I never had any formal training on leadership. Most of what I know I have learned from God and from His Word. I believe God is the ultimate source of truth and love. As illustrated on the book cover, *there is no better place to grow than in the palm of God's hand.* I would ask each of you to seek Him in order to learn more of what we discussed here. Have fun learning and may God touch all you do.

YOUR PERSONAL ACTION PLAN

Action Plan

Focus Area:

The Better Situation:

The Current Situation: (strengths and weaknesses)

Action Plan Items / Behavior Change

1) _____

2) _____

3) _____

Let Go		Take Hold
Mind		
Change: _____	⇨	_____
Thoughts	⇨	
Beliefs _____	⇨	_____
Assumptions	⇨	
Feelings _____		_____

Printed in the United States
65434LVS00001B/217-243